'The Scream'—among others—are among the best I've read in ages. This is a book that's hard to put down. It's difficult not to feel utterly changed after having read it." —ROWAN RICARDO PHILLIPS

"An intensely vulnerable book: vulnerable in its questions, in its openness to the reality of others, those who are present and those who are not. Even as it interrogates the fraught limitations of these attempts, it delves deeply into the challenge of attuning the body and language toward alertness, inviting us into a series of deftly made lyric rooms that allow cohabitation with strangeness and strangers, with the dead, with loss, with absence, with unknowing. Joudah has been writing essential poetry for some time, but few books of American poetry seem to me as essential as this one: it is forging a lyric that works at the crosscurrents of reportage, myth, and dream where falsely imagined boundaries—of gender, nation, family—fray and unfold, and there are possibilities other than 'to go mad among the mad / or go it alone.' Joudah's gifts for articulating the intersections of bewilderment, tenderness, rage, and grief are fully alive here. These poems blaze into the visionary." —MARY SZYBIST

"Joudah's masterful *Footnotes in the Order of Disappearance* combines ecstasy and irony, or perhaps conveys an ecstatic sense of irony that trusts the imagination's associations. The poet's words, scooped from an encyclopedic range of topics and references, make encores and double swerves, through which we learn to learn and learn to unlearn as well. The poet's exilic experience and his profession as a physician, his sites of testimony, offer him and us multiple prisms to move outward in the world and inward into the self, in a reserved tone that preserves ache and joy intact. Joudah's mission is perhaps to spiritualize our minds, and to catch the heart in its deepest modes of thinking, and the outcome is lyric of the highest order." —KHALED MATTAWA

"Can a doctor diagnose the body politic? Yes, if he is also a poet. Joudah examines his subject with an eye both clinical and caring, alert to the symptoms we don't recognize or won't admit we have. His language is like crystal: patterned, prismatic, sharp. We travel: from the hospitals of Houston to the streets of Paris, from the pines of Aleppo to the banks of the Rhone. Palestine is everywhere and nowhere, like sorrow, circulating through this collection like blood. The poet, clear-eyed and truthful even to himself, identifies our choices: 'To go mad among the mad / or go it alone'; offers his treatment: 'I sent up the part of me that was light'; conveys the results: 'Sometimes people survive in spite of us.'" —EVIE SHOCKLEY

FOOTNOTES

in the

ORDER

of

DISAPPEARANCE

Also by Fady Joudah

POETRY COLLECTIONS

The Earth in the Attic

Alight

Textu

TRANSLATIONS

The Butterfly's Burden by Mahmoud Darwish

If I Were Another by Mahmoud Darwish

Like a Straw Bird It Follows Me by Ghassan Zaqtan

A Map of Signs and Scents (with Khaled Mattawa)
by Amjad Nasser

The Silence That Remains by Ghassan Zaqtan

FOOTNOTES

in the

ORDER

of

DISAPPEARANCE

poems

FADY JOUDAH

MILKWEED EDITIONS

Published 2018 by Milkweed Editions
Cover design by Mary Austin Speaker
Cover photo by Liu Nian / iStock
Author photo by Cybele Knowles

Milkweed Editions, an independent nonprofit publisher, gratefully acknowledges sustaining support from the Jerome Foundation; the Lindquist & Vennum Foundation; the McKnight Foundation; the National Endowment for the Arts; the Target Foundation; and other generous contributions from foundations, corporations, and individuals. Also, this activity is made possible by the voters of Minnesota through a Minnesota State Arts Board Operating Support grant, thanks to a legislative appropriation from the arts and cultural heritage fund, and a grant from Wells Fargo. For a full listing of Milkweed Editions supporters, please visit milkweed.org.

Library of Congress Cataloging-in-Publication Data

Names: Joudah, Fady, 1971- author.
Title: Footnotes in the order of disappearance : poems / Fady Joudah.
Description: First Edition. | Minneapolis, Minnesota: Milkweed Editions, 2018.
Identifiers: LCCN 2017036821 | ISBN 9781571315014 (pbk. : alk. paper)
Classification: LCC PS3610.O679 A6 2018 | DDC 811/.6--dc23
LC record available at https://lccn.loc.gov/2017036821

CONTENTS

I.

II. Sagittal Views: A Collaboration with Golan Haji

III.

You ask about the effects of my works on others. If I may wax ironical, that is a masculine question. Men always want to be terribly influential. . . . No. I want to understand. And if others understand—in the same sense that I have understood—that gives me a sense of satisfaction, like feeling at home.

HANNAH ARENDT

Sometimes they arrest you while you're committing a dream.

MAHMOUD DARWISH

I.

THE MAGIC OF APRICOT

The magic of apricot
when the scent is flesh and descent is one bite
and you're a Moor speaking Chinese

The magic of apricot
the last time you saw home whole
a child and a lotus tree
laden with figs in the fall

What Lazarus looks like in the brain
or what the brain looks like on Lazarus

The magic of apricot
my bare feet and the plasma core of the world
smeared by human hands

The magic of apricot says
no one's ever nude on radiology film
and I'm grateful for my nipples
ripening early in frost

The magic of apricot
quotes those who've quoted you
changes what solid means
with two fingers
shakes the stamen sprays the anthers

A vocalist who doesn't sing
convulses his body
negative capability a capella style

The magic of apricot may well keep us alive
a little while longer than unnecessary

Andalus is also Petra
the maggots of place
healers of severance and decay
Machu Picchu sleeps at night
and hustles by day

The magic of apricot
my daughter blurts out
the three unprompted words
"I love you"
in Arabic one

Apricot
let there be digital archives
hector the microfilm

Apricot
the falafel of truth
and the truth of falafel

the stuff of novels

the truffle of return

the ordinariness of scallions

we paid for the memory

A soldier's yellow sclera, blue skin, as those whose skin wasn't
blue said his was. Otherwise he seemed well. Not much more
than contact isolation, the solitary confinement a contagious
person suffers from their contagium. Use your own towels,
silverware, and poop away from where others poop. In rick-
ety rack barracks, they came begging for basic meds we kept
like black gold in plastic containers the size of houseplant pots
before planting. I returned, could return. When I say God Is
Great I mean God Is Greater. On a Houston Sunday morning
at Empire Café on Westheimer Road, I read aloud two short
amorous verses to my wife over breakfast while we sipped Irish
coffee. Delighted she exclaimed "Allahu Akbar" and the whole
place turned its doll head toward us. The moment was brief.
An audiovisual specialist helped me to set up my PowerPoint
presentation for a medical audience that awaited my travelogue.
I included the photo of the soldier's face as record of the jaun-
dice. I'd asked for his permission and he granted it with lucid
lack of understanding. The lens captured only his eyes and nose
where, as I clicked, a fly landed and became our third. When
the specialist came across the snap he was ebullient, pointed to
the fly and said "The icing on the cake."

PROGRESS NOTES

The age of portrait is drugged. Beauty
is symmetry so rare it's a mystery.
My left eye is smaller than my right,
my big mouth shows my nice teeth perfectly
aligned like Muslims in prayer.
My lips an accordion. Each sneeze
a facial thumbprint. One corner
of my mouth hangs downward when I want
to hold a guffaw hostage. Bell's palsy perhaps
or what Mark Twain said about steamboat piloting,
that a doctor's unable to look upon the blush
in a young beauty's face without thinking
it could be a fever, a malar rash,
a butterfly announcing a wolf. Can I lie
facedown now as cadavers posed
on first anatomy lesson? I didn't know mine
was a woman until three weeks later
we turned her over. Out of reverence
there was to be no untimely exposure of donors,
our patrons who were covered in patches
of scrubs-green dish towels,
and by semester's end we were sick of all that,
tossed mega livers and mammoth hearts
into lab air and caught them. My body
was Margaret. That's what the death certificate said
when it was released before finals. The cause
of her death? Nothing memorable,
frail old age. But the colonel on table nineteen
with an accessory spleen had put a bullet through
his temple, a final prayer. Not in entry or exit
were there skull cracks to condemn the house

of death, no shattered glass in the brain,
only a smooth tunnel of deep violet that bloomed
in concentric circles. The weekends were lonely.
He had the most beautiful muscles
of all 32 bodies that were neatly arranged,
zipped up as if a mass grave had been disinterred.
Or when unzipped and facing the ceiling
had cloth over their eyes as if they'd just been executed.
Gray silver hair, chiseled countenance,
he was sixty-seven, a veteran of more than one war.
I had come across that which will end me, ex-
tend me, at least once, without knowing it.

ECHO #1

One right move
no place to go

we goat through tombs
eviscerated of their residents

It was lovely
to see you defeated after dinner

with splanchnic blood
shunted from your brain's hollering terrain

Lovely the wet ashes
of your voice the evagination

of palm-sized cantaloupe
our conversation

of a year ago has changed
the body has changed

our guest
that hosts us

THANK YOU

Professor who ran the anatomy department and was a preacher's son. You were an ex-preacher yourself, abandoned the cloth after you divorced your wife and married your lover. Thank you for your hands that a surgeon would incise for, your mouth for transfiguration, enunciation, you were kind to me.

At the end of each year you held a memorial service for the cadavers. Afterlife subscribers or not, and down to the wires that held them together, they would all be cremated.

The fuss about the body interred isn't the same as about the body discovered. I threw my name in the hat. I'd recite verses from the Quran in Arabic and you'd follow in English. I proposed, you accepted. I had my own bilingual copy. I forget which verses I chose but they were generous to the faithful. I put on my best Barry White and went into a trance.

"You didn't notice it," my friend later asked me, "the discomfort in the room when you read?" I didn't, I told him. All I heard and felt was how you, Professor, delivered. Every syllable, word.

MAQAM OF PALM TREES

His amphibian torso-
to-leg ratio a frog's

or imitation (fiddler) crab
soluble salty rubber of two waters

at the confluence of steady eddy synapse
In a museum's dark room

his triceps' fat pressed to hers
she in her movement

he in his stillness
what the moving know about stillness

the still don't know . . . She asks
Are you a Sufi?

Is all my longing
born equal to your ears

the devil's a devoted angel
with personality disorder

or what will we do tonight? He says
I'll make us coffee and tea

we'll play chutes and ladders
and in the morning

we'll feed a bale of turtles
and a bevy of swans

our bagels on a deck
settled in lake-drought mud

where I was born . . . She says
Then maybe a heron will join

and leave us a calamus
so big it can wound

December evening, smoke in the rain, awn of the rain, from virga to drizzle, a glimpse of horses through large wooden doors, trunks immortal, a manège (which in Dutch rhymes with Malaysia), warmbloods in the training ring. Seven in a trotting circle spun up to a canter, motion sustained. Round and round twenty-eight hooves tap dance twenty-eight lungs. All women riders. The da Vinci shoulders, breasts, thighs, fibers, fascicles. Foam in stalactites from equine jaws more exhausted than a crossroad. Steam rising to the roof. The sinews of their hearts. The women were one, horses one. For miles and miles rooted to the ring's rail I rode along. (From one body to the next I crossed as in a single body the bridges are endless.) The riders dismounted, led the horses to their stalls, drew vapor clouds idly away from the eye of the fugue. One rider stayed on her horse. Her smile held me. Her chest was still rising, falling, but when she spoke the air was well at ease. "How long have you been riding for?" she asked me. "I don't know how," I said. All the horses I never rode, their magnetic fields filled with souls of past riders and horses' past souls, even the plastic ones I used to line up on the sill. "Oh," she said, though it's conceivable she was asking me about something altogether different. My heart's a doe's. A doe's made for running away.

IST LOVE

When God began you she
said to me one spring afternoon in bed
God began

with your hands
a woman's hands

And when God reached your wrists
God made the rest of you man

BEANSTALK

I was twelve when I asked my older brother about the clitoris. He told me it was a structure on the outside of a woman's vagina that was the size of a chickpea. If you hold it between your fingers, he said, a woman instantly melts, and he made a soft gesture of rubbing his index finger and thumb together, as if he were dusting off flour after eating a piece of bread, or stroking the wing of a moth. He'd never seen one, I was sure of it, but I could sense he wasn't lying. He'd felt one maybe in the stairwell of some building that wasn't fully housed on the campus where we lived in Riyadh. He had a reputation for being a Don Juan, which got him in trouble with the local boys. But the size of a chickpea? When I went to medical school the dimension never left my mind. If his fingers were accurate, objective, not subject to the delirium of pleasure at fourteen, then there's only one explanation: he must have encountered a girl with clitoromegaly. A cadaver had a large penis in our anatomy lab the first year of medical school. The tiniest woman in class, who went on to become a pathologist, could not get over the size of it. She kept saying, "Look at the size of it! How can that fit?" Two years earlier, while taking premed anatomy, when it was penis time, and the cloth was removed, I don't know why I uttered these words under my breath: "So small yet so many troubles." A classmate who was standing right behind me approached me after class to tell me she was moved by my remark. She had been a victim of rape. I was stunned. She wanted to talk. She told me she lived in a house in the middle of Nowhere Road, in Athens, Georgia.

COLORED RINGS

I submit to the machine
I have a shredder in my office

I'm a terra rist a maqam of earth
and when I die I want to go to Saturn

Thank you for dreaming of me
for waking up to remember what you dreamed
I never wake up when I dream of you

What woke you?
Was it someone else's body

our small thrill and secret
for safe travel in unspilled blood?

Thank you for rolling
your tobacco for me to smoke
the closest my lips came to your fingertips

and your tongue's glue
to the air in my lungs

And for the beer
one after another

in the viscidity of a mafioso city
without electricity in summer

until whenever we spoke

THE HOUR OF THE GRACKLE

The hour of the grackle, common,
indigo, icteric-eyed New World

passerine, is sunset
charting a map of the united

airways on in-flight magazine,
our skyscraper roofs in the business district

the launchpads for these winged spiders
flinging bituminous webs, nystagmic

fish schools in air, ribbon
dancers, a harras

in rush hour light, and no bird shit to rain
on your parade

                            ✦

The hour of the grackle, and a mother
not menopausal, solitary with endgame lung

tumor in a foreign country
and what makes one foreign:

she hasn't seen her son for three or five
exilic or immigrant years,

citizen or national stints, a keyword
a thrombus dislodges

in heart or head
for infarction's infraction

◆

The hour of the grackle, common, declines
my offer for an interview,

its raucous song Hitchcockian
in parking lots and on treetops,

blackened shoots, a surfeit
optical illusion if judged

over highway as the birds
subpoena Bacchus

◆

Then in cornfields
we waste them, their decrement attritional

over decades, to defend our maize
that we dump at sea

to subsidize the sea, or ship
to camps we globetrot for almsgiving

◆

The hour of the grackle
in my city's sunset

a daily reprieve
in fenestrated sky

FOOTNOTES TO A PICTURE

Where "it was Psyche, his soul, his fixed contemplation,"
the renowned psychiatrist said of his friend's pose,
where during the final decade of the poet's life, the butterfly
was classified on the Indian subcontinent,
where *Leptosia nina*, "wandering snowflake," takes to low
fragile flight, its wings tipping grass,
where in twilight he sat down clad in cardigan
in the city of bromance, where a plump
cardboard moth had synthetically alighted
on his outstretched index, the visible rubber band
in daguerreotype, the lepidoptera in equilibrium
and on its hind wings some words, not his, housed
in the Library of Congress, where "Yes,
that was an actual moth, the picture
is substantially literal, we were good friends"
during my "in-and-out of taming,
or fraternizing with, some of the insects,"
where their swarms and migratory shadows
and the current they ride up I ride up,
where it isn't all water when it rains.

NATIONAL PARK

We saw a lot more of them dead than alive
the living diffident

by the side of the road
as the far-off mountains flanked and intoxicated
the speedometer into saunter

The dead were interspersed on the asphalt
their poor vision uncorrected
by their auditory keenness
like a blind spot in a poet

and their fender-mangled corpses
were occasionally ripped in two
before vultures reached them

In our rental van
we left no mother bereft
and orphaned no piglets

Turkey buzzards and American vultures
were the javelinas' gift to us

red and black scavengers
that perched on ranchland fences
the full span of highway

they'd circle above in diminishing downward spirals
or flinch at each other's puffs and swells
or away from incoming vehicles

Still they shared the dead among them
as we sometimes share our dead
when we love our dead

Javelina the Arabic word
for mountain in its root

and then the mountain
coming closer to an ear
became a spear

PLETHORA

About the praise I dish your way
jail's the comeuppance of a liar poet

My only want is your content and if I hold
another want may I never be granted it

Each full moon is born of a crescent
yet what's a full moon got?

Vitiligo
and the morning sees me with eyes of dew

a fever breaking out
on your integument

On your skin exanthem
is a pasture of anemones

Because you're one of them
I love my enemies

EPITHALAMION

We hold the present responsible for my hand
in your hand, my thumb

as aspirin leaves a painless bruise, our youth
immemorial in a wormhole for silence

to rescue us, the heart free at last
of the tongue (the dream, the road) upon

which our hours reside together alone,
that this is love's profession, our scents

on pillows displace our alphabet to grass
with fidelity around our wrists

and breastbones, thistle and heather.
And this steady light, angular

through the window, is no amulet
to store in a dog-eared book.

A body exits all pages to be
inscribed on another, itself.

Morning slept well. The fruit vendor—an immigrant in a Paris street market whose name I can access but don't recall—sliced a peach and called out to passersby, city dwellers, tourists to try this heart of his, not too sour, not too sweet, ripe, ready, his bare hands looked as dry as can be expected, the pocketknife blade clean as well. Many refused. A few reached out and let his quartered peach fall unto their fingertips furled like flowers. They ate his offering then walked off with or without shaking their heads, No thank you or Yes but no. You waited as you chewed then picked four fruits, one for each chamber. He said, "Gorgeous, you're the one who's mended my heart."

CHAMBER MUSIC

You say thalamos, I say thalamus
and hypostasis is invention
as the mother of need. For everything a body

and in our version of Willie Pete
few babies make it out of nativity complete.

To seduce you, reduce you to myself, corrode
myself at the anode for you, tremors
for holy water, Hagar's hands and feet

I pant and plead, "Gather,
gather," in a dead language.

The dead split in two. One camp
house-warms their graves with the living's
carnation and chrysanthemum, while in the other

children hide and seek in ice cream coolers
of vendors turned morticians.

To wait out burial
the body sits in the needle's eye,
not chasm but chiasm

that holds off incoming thread
and feeds another through.

I'm staying right there. You go
look for horses in the peace
forged between beasts.

I'm staying with all I have on loan
as tone flickers its penultimate

oxygen pair, you go be the beginning.
It was already the beginning
when love was one of its traits.

that startled me while I was on my knees depositing my son one morning in the kindergarten line stationed in the cafeteria/theatre/gym where he sits facing the stage amid twelve rows of kids waiting for the bell, that pierce came from behind, from a boy with bloody nose, his fingers bearing the coagulating fluid of his life. I, a doctor with warm sweat invading my pores, turned toward him and cupped his face as in a prayer. A mother, not his mother, came with paper towel, wiped off his nose, and left as fast as she came into the scene. The evidence erased, the boy stopped crying. I asked him what happened. He pointed to the boy behind him. I questioned the accused and he seized into absence. A nurse came and took Abel. I stroked Cain's hair, his frightened stare, gorgeous eyes, he was beautiful.

THE LIVING ARE THE MINORITY

The river of words in the land of the dead is narrow

a trickle through a wadi that couldn't submerge a duck's foot

a river not made of the living's tears

the dead don't cry

and mindful of dehydration

they speak what they drink

and wave to their ventriloquists

FOOTNOTES TO A SONG

Echo has no compass: we trace each other's dermatomes

No ecstasy without betrayal: not all who live in flames are saints

Great art needs no nation: in memory country size is one

Great nations need great art: soliloquy a mother tongue

The surface tension of a Jesus bug: opiates me

We reach a cemetery: to each a cemetery

What is seen ends: even if its ending isn't seen

Tethered to a trope: great nations need great despair

Great despair: needs nary a nation

My grief for a grievance: we're radiocarbon

Your grief for a grievance: we're mitochondriacs

{ }

II.

SAGITTAL VIEWS

A collaboration with Golan Haji

A silent feeling of an invisible punishment or one seen through cataracts, a sentence that isn't meted out and doesn't end; some cuts run deeper than speech: writing may exit the cage but the cage remains and grows, or am I speaking of the life of a footnoter; I always hold back from writing in the margins of the clearest sentences: those that lost their status as feeling once they were excised by skillful hands wielding sharp instruments, a manufacture of refraction; a while back I saw a commercial in black and white for a detergent: its customer was imprisoned in a soap bubble that can't be breached, a second transparent skin he can't exit before the commercial ends; I think it was inspired by a Chinese man who was jailed for life as a child inside an iron ball: as he grew the penalty—the ball grew until it was no longer possible to tell his blood from the ball's rust, and I can't remember what he was punished for; no silence offers answers:

IN THE GARDEN

We watched fish navigate the canals.
In one pool a fish in its orange jumpsuit
floated to the green surface under the shadows of giant
linden and horse chestnut. The ducks
were alarmed. Other fish were quick
to deflect their trajectory after the softest brush
with the deceased. I waited. No seagull came. Death vacated
a circle around the departed, like an antibiotic disc
in a petri dish diffusing its minimum inhibitory capacity.
We walked for a long stretch, reached the flamingo reserve
then headed to the beach. Our daughter
took some Mediterranean sand in her mouth
before we rode the train. On the banks of the Rhone
fires sent up a large smoke cloud
that began to rain. Tender ash
fell cool over the towns. At the station
the skin of people waiting to board
had changed tone.

AFTER WINE

Over dinner we spoke of the game of recurrence dissolving
into an old dog's tail, loquacious desire far from the borders
of the body, yet is the body's. What's inside and doesn't come
out to skin or what's outside and doesn't touch us. Victims,
we told ourselves, will inherit the future one day, but souls
will linger distant from redemption. Don't follow the signage
and keep your eyes on the phrase. News of the explosion will
hang around. The hell of pictures on the web. Faces of the dead
on Facebook will wait for your walk home. A woman who
awakened your first lust when you were a kid was killed in the
morning while talking to her sister on the phone. First a blast
then stillness. You were late to dinner. You had lost your way to
the restaurant. You couldn't have known she had just died, and
what you thought were Klee's paintings in the gallery clawing
your afternoon nerves was her calling your name one last time.
In the neighborhood of your boyhood, you rise with tractors
and loaders, start your engines, clear the infinite wake with only
the living to show for. Isn't that what so hurt Nabokov about
the Bolsheviks? Not the real estate, private tutors, governesses,
or inheritance, but the loss of childhood? Listening to music
you feel better. Long ago in Amuda one of your uncles fell in
love with a woman. He strung for her an erotic necklace he
sang whenever he was drunk and unconcerned with the truths
of the world. Her brothers put a bounty on his head. Decades
passed in Damascus and that woman's granddaughter fell in
love with your uncle's grandson. He was also a singer, sang of
Guevara and Paul Robeson, went to Iraq and came back dead.
His shrine was his body in a coffin in a boat that crossed the
Tigris from east to west.

I, THE SOLE WITNESS TO MY DESPAIR, DECLARE

Meditation? I search for a clown I kill
and repeatedly revive, resuscitate
per the most recent update in the science
of purgatory. I am not one of Sparta's elderly
banished to the mountains. I will squeeze me
some fresh orange juice. Solutions are euphemisms
for new binds and delirium can't be apprehended.
It agglutinates like rubber, like histogenesis,
and love doesn't console
the sorrows I inherited in my skull.
In my left temple and jaw ants wake up.
The bus bell rings police hooves on the sidewalk
outside my door. What kind
of domestication school is reality? A beaver
is building a home in my blood. Sweet clot
of wakefulness, what is mercy?
To go mad among the mad
or go it alone.

The boat was loaded on a truck. The truck took me to the border. I was by myself hiding in the hull's chine and emerged holding a two-sided oar. At the checkpoint, hordes of refugees in riot control formation without the gear. They were asking the questions. "Who wrote this book?" or "Where did this phrase first appear?" To pass through I had to match quotes and author names to book titles. Sometimes the refugees got specific about characters or incidents. And if I answered one query correctly they released others like clay pigeons for my faltering rifle. They were vituperative but let me through once a look of shame had overwhelmed my fraudulent visage. They were well read. Their city was deserted. You were taking a bucket shower in a roofless thatch-stall under the full gaze of stars, and your matted hair was a raft. We said nothing as our lips simulated union before you panicked. "A monster's coming," you said, "speak, I implore you, now that you're no longer a continent apart."

"WISSWASS"

Encephalopathy. Unbidden thoughts. Intrusive. Identical molecular weight of riffraff. The utterance of brass, or *ras*, the family of genes whose mutation sometimes activates cancer. More Rasputin than Rasta but not quite either. And in some dictionaries it's the ringing of gold. Paranoia or hallucination also apply. To dream perchance to emaciate. Those who fall prey to it console themselves with early saints. Saint Sebastian, for example. He was tied by his long hair to a tree trunk while arrows broke into and against his waist. Before he was a martyr he was an urchin or a porcupine. He was buried twice.

LAST NIGHT'S FEVER, THIS MORNING'S MURDER

I read your name among the numbered, nearly
called you to console you of your own passing. Thirty
summers ago, susurrant wheat guided me
to a wounded sand grouse chick that had punctuated
the dirt with its blood. I couldn't identify its wound
or didn't look for it before I made an empty can
of camel lard its nest. The metal shone
in the sun like the shards of broken mirrors we kept
in the basement. I waited alone at the bus stop
south of the lone remaining poplar
we buried you under, in what remains
of the courtyard. Your house stood in front
of the ice cutters' shop where blocks
came out in burlap and headed to the harvester.
Like a tortoise I waited for the tortoise bus
under the balcony whose door killed you
while your kids were sleeping.

Amira, did you hear Jigar's voice under the rubble?
Is it true the rescuers finished him off, a hospice act
or is he still alive down there? Your death was white
like sleep, like salt, like dust mixed with flour
sacked and loaded on trucks. Thirty summers ago
a family photo caught fire. I was the only one
who survived the burning. By dawn your laugh
rings in my ears among Aleppo's pine.

In the hole in front of your house I lie and extend
my arms up to your balcony's door, a long rope
of handkerchiefs, a magic act for beginners,

my grandmother's braid which we didn't send
with her to the grave. We cut and kept it.

Had you left your windows open, your door, Amira,
we wouldn't have had this wreckage of your rooms
out in the street for all to see. Not the poplar trunks
and branches that fell like hammers on our camping gear.
And not the shattered glass of farewell empty of its drink.

Did I tell you what happened to Ali who escaped
Iraq to Syria? His door also killed him. Some windfall
for an angry boy who volleyed our shoes
into the neighbor's house one New Year's Eve.
But in summer song returns. In summer
we sing a love song your husband used to sing
in wheat fields. And songs return to children
terrified of trucks and destinies. Children
with straw brooms who shoo away wasps that hover
around squash rind. In summer
Yazidis roll their cantaloupe carts
in our streets. And in song
there's a cool fire.

Amira, tonight
a moon will rise like a watermelon crescent
a Kurd wishes for his sleeping daughter
just before the story ends.

Meditation? I can't tell my Buddhist prayers
from my scammed being. If only
reality didn't lay siege to my head
I'd celebrate existence. Across the street
cruel people gain entry through the corner
of my eye. They curse beggars
who don't speak their language and the beggars
go on singing for them. Chatter is a profession
and seclusion is the lady of the house.
I think of Chekhov's sneeze. A spark
that illumines my brain's occluded ducts.
Can a waterfall wear a rein? I am the rusting nail
that dreams of a scored white pill. Anxiety
is a short corridor to the end of things
but the end of things is endless. Survival
opens onto illness. And the unjust
are pious when they sleep.

For decades you thought you were a Scorpio until your sister informed you, according to one birth certificate, you were a Sagittarius.

I can hear your laugh: the one I took for vestige joy filled with trifles among decimated lives. I can hear your laugh when our friend, who inhabited the earth as a metal horse for thirty years, felt she'd been living in the wrong body all along. But when her search led her to the wooden monkey, she resurrected her equine past.

Centaurs and sphinxes were evolution's idea in a human mind no longer hallucinatory yet longing for hallucination. Lucretius was right, you said. He saw the step where the math didn't add up in an equation that had gone on for pages to a conclusion. The method remains unknown but feels correct. Its seduction bewilders until another truth takes hold in substantial numbers. The numbers are invariably wrong and the answer is never one.

Then we solve for it again. Your mom was born in the maiden year of the zodiac of aerial bombing. Her town was among the chosen. My mom was born in the constellation of armistice. What bones do the planets comminute?

Before we met, you and I had been in love
with the same verse: "My heart in life
is my body in death." You knew it
years before I did. Every face has kiss lines.

IN A CEMETERY UNDER A SOLITARY WALNUT TREE THAT CROWS

had planted and whose seeds are hollow
I found a needle and with it

I dug a well
dug and dug until I struck ink

The needle wove fabric for bodies it had injected with song
I painted the well's walls with quicklime and couldn't climb out

There was sun there was moonlight that came into my sleep
I stored leaves and bark but rain washed away my words

A lantern came down on a rope that a girl held
I sent up the part of me that was light

{ }

III.

That syphilis leads to deafness isn't enough
for Beethoven to have died of it. There's Baudelaire's
spleen and Nietzsche's tempo, or did Emily
suffer from seizures? Did Muhammad? If so

were hers absence and his simple or partial complex? Unlikely
the grand mal type since horror makes itself known.

Dear reader, how might two authors with differing epilepsies write?
Make a documentary on postictal testimony. On bleeding
George Washington to death as part of his treatment plan.

Those who were afflicted with collagen disease
have already been alluded to in a previous section.
Construct an ıbıd:

After presiding over mosquitoes Walter Reed pulled a Houdini.
King Louis's anal fistula was heaven-sent
for surgical technique. As it was probably during combat
that Sultan Baibers acquired a tear in his pupillary sphincter.

Her eyes were blue, her iris orange. JFK's
adrenal disease, that bronze we took for gold.
And Lord Jeffrey, my smallpox Lord.

As for Familial Mediterranean Fever it belongs to everyone.
Humanitarian medicine is infectious, its donors stem cell.

Those who received the body were young. Trauma
practice was young, droning about all that talk
of mental illness in 500 words or less.

Name a schizophrenic on the dream list.
Your favorite Lou Gehrig or *The Madness
of King George*, one of my favorite flicks. I saw it
with a lover I lost, her eyes were hazel, their waters green.

Now repeat after me
the three objects I asked you to hold.

For I never had a cat I called my own.
For he ravaged the neighbor's chickens for monk brains.
For they kidnapped him and he never returned.

KOHL

-May you roam in your coquetry

-May beauty make you monarch over me

-I'm lachrymose no more

-A Sahara weeps its molten iris

-Would one spare their prey when their prey are in coitus?

-Would drone would artillery?

-Testicles are low-hanging colocynths

-Ruins are tattoos of earth

-And lightning a monk's lantern

-A camel hump is a Roman arch

-An oil rig an ibex in head butt

-And a praying mantis a reflex hammer

-On your elbows and knees

-Wrists and Achilles' heels

BODY OF MEANING

Is this how she spent her mind's days
worn out by the no-wonder of it all, injustice
a consciousness so old it's impossible
to PET-scan without a bolus of antimatter?

She's a Jedi
and I'm one of seven sleepers in a cave
with our dog. When we woke
the dog was first out the door.

The soul doesn't roam
outside the body anymore. If history's
a phoenix then what options
when the two phoenixes meet?

Medusa's mother:
she sought help for her daughter, a young bride
who was twice married and straightaway

twice divorced. The daughter couldn't speak
or smile or turn and face you without twitching
into fine-motor hell. She had

a bulging stare. With no pills
to down in a swig and no radioiodine
around, her mother wove her a wig.

Dear poem, today I learned that the man who'd made it to his wedding wearing only one shoe (having dropped the other while running away from soldiers) was caught days after his matrimony, sentenced to three years in prison.

A jailbird whose sole visitor was his young aunt. The penal system didn't consider her a direct blood relative. She used his sister's ID. Once a week she visited her nephew with a large fruit basket, reported back to his mother (her sister) and kissed her cloven heart.

Whenever a soldier asked the sister-aunt to state her name, she'd spill the fruit basket on the floor. The soldier would lose his cool, shout, and mutilate her mother tongue, "gather, gather, clean, clean," then in disgust toss back her ID without verification, shoo her inside to spare the place from turning into a fruit stand.

Like clockwork she kept at it until officers recognized her face, looked the other way. A couple of years after the jailbird's release, his wife (who had made him tea with sage on their wedding night) found herself clutching their second child as warplanes bombed the city again.

She darted outside the house into bare space. Her husband reached her in an opening between two rubble heaps. She was unable to move, her newborn alive, latched on to her dry nipple. She's in wheelchair now. Her body refuses to ambulate. A translational injury of all that pummeled earth.

She also refuses to speak. Some of the women, in what remained of the district, told the mother-in-law it would be OK if her son sought a new bride, but the husband's mother said, "Why should he? She waited for him once. It's his turn to wait. Besides, they're happy. It's you who can't see it when you visit them for tea.

"She may not speak but she always sings. What she wants to say to him she finds in the lyrics of songs, old and new. She can carry a tune. And he replies in kind."

NONTERMINAL

No shards
         where one is bound to no place in the first place

      all shards
               we were clear on that from the beginning

Absence is always sudden to hear your voice
                    once more more

echo than shrapnel qualia of the forbidden

regenerates its wounds into
                        hydra or lizard tail
Touch me
      I'm alive again

there isn't enough time or proximity
for your essence or mine   to vanish

we'll remain
         fire and ice who turn to glass
that doesn't shatter

mercury
         if it shatters

POEM FOR GODOT

My dog, the mosquitoes
that siphon my blood,

the cucumbers, each
have their horoscope.

Do cucumbers bear
the stars of their flowers?

It's the zygote
that marks me. My dog,

a designer mutt, a Pisces,
my favorite type of folks,

hates water, loves mud.
The azalea in the garden

bloomed a Leo, its seeds
ascended a Taurus sky.

And St. Francis's birthday
is unknown though his zodiac is

his wolf's. Giovanni, shipwrecked
before I reached Jerusalem

I talked with the birds.
Are you the hoopoe

or the simurgh? In Egypt
I shared my nights and rations

with a canid: everywhere
we went we met no witness.

ECHO #14

I say "egg" you say "imago"
where the Moor would be without Iago,
and when in Texas, don't mess with the magnesium
we already messed with the manganese.

Can you play Mississippi for me?
One Mississippi two Mississippi goddamn.
I ask "What do elephants think of the stars?"
You ask "What do fisheyes or dragonflies see?"

Then a phoenix attempts to login
our kisses. Your user ID:
"In my name's erasure and my body's form"
(a butterfly bone in the mind). My password:

"I asked about you and you answered, You"
(in the shavings of a sharpened pencil).

"I've never been," I said to my friend who'd just come back from there. "Oh you should definitely go," she said. "The original Palestine is in Illinois." She went on, "A pastor was driven out by Palestine's people and it hurt him so badly he had to rename somewhere else after it. Or maybe it goes back to a 17th century Frenchman who traveled with his vision of milk and honey, or the nut who believed in dual seeding." "What's that?" I asked. "That's when an egg is fertilized by two sperm," she said. "Is that even viable?" I asked. "It is," she said, "on rare occasions, though nothing guarantees the longevity of the resulting twins." She spoke like a scientist but was a professor of the humanities at heart. "Viability," she added, "depends on the critical degree of disproportionate defect distribution for a miracle to occur. If there is life, only one twin lives." That night we went to the movies looking for a good laugh. It was a Coen brothers' feature whose unheralded opening scene rattled off Palestine this, Palestine that and the other, it did the trick. We were granted the right to exist. It must have been there and then that my wallet slipped out of my jeans' back pocket and under the seat. The next morning, I went back. With a flashlight that the manager had lent me I found the wallet unmoved. This was the second time in a year that I'd lost and retrieved this modern cause of sciatica in men. Months earlier it was at a lily pond I'd gone hiking to with the same previously mentioned friend. It was around twilight. Another woman, going in with her boyfriend as we were coming out, picked it up, put it in her little backpack, and weeks later texted me the photo of his kneeling and her standing with right hand over mouth, to thwart the small bird in her throat from bursting. If the bird escapes, the cord is severed, and the heart plummets. She didn't want the sight of joy caught in her teeth. He sat his phone camera on its pod and set it in lapse mode, she wrote in her text to me. I welled up. She would become a bride and my wallet was part of the proposal. This made me a token of their bliss, though I'm not sure how her fiancé might feel about my intrusion, if he'd care at all. "It's a special wallet," I texted back. "It's been with me for the better part of two decades ever since a good friend got it for me as a present." "He was from Ohio," I turned and said to my film mate who was listening to my story. "Ohio?" She seemed surprised. "Yes," I replied quizzically. "There's also a Palestine in Ohio," she said. "Barely anyone lives there anymore. All of them barely towns off country roads."

SOME THINGS

Some things are better when they fall apart
natural selection
random selection
ashes from a hole in the ground

Some things I wanted to be good when I fall apart
secrets compressed into a fracture
a spine locates to prop open a mouth

Some things are monasteries
my auricle a hem
that's been moth-eaten

Some things atrophy
catastrophe
rapture
my position in the fifth column of your ringlets

Some things proliferate
the dead for years in my sleep
like radioactive wolves
in droplets of dew

And the God
who was the dog
a woman wouldn't exchange for heaven

THE FLOOR IS YOURS

My chickenpox hotel
your machinegun pointillism

My bamboo branch
severed but nimble name
in the air of two alphabets
Picassos in bull-light routine

Your mantis
welded on a pole with spiral staircase
my romance
between pillager and villager
timed and timely

intensity inversely
proportional to frequency
the chickadees in your voice

the thrush in my mouth
our polymers of I skipping
their archipelago stones

Your touchscreen
my ringtone heart

Your mahogany gift bag
puffed with confetti
our songs as gauze
for a new island

BLOODLINE

A beetle with phosphorescent indigo wings
I had assumed were radium yellow
cascaded down the glass of God to the table
by your right arm

and I said that a painter friend of mine
with inflammatory vessels in her mind
(an ailment whose choice of flesh
is blood-vessel muscle)

had told me that indigo
is like the untranslatable in every language:

synonym overlap too low for coefficient,
Rothko's chromatography
or electrophoresis in and out of his Chapel

—A Mexican rabbi doctor from Aleppo
had recently shared with me
that he'd seen the work
but didn't get the art in it

I told him he'd have to go into it knowing Rothko
didn't see the spirit bright
and didn't see it hurtful either

though it could be that it's Rothko retro days
and Twombly's mausoleum across the street
under a Whitman oak
and the city's grackles at sunset

on treetops and ledges
on traffic lights and wires
along feeders and highways
wild song and murmuration

Then the rabbi said that once as a boy
his father had reproached him for mocking Arabic
which his father spoke and loved

"And my father knew love" he said
"So maybe that's indigo" I said—

You said your beetle had landed
and was wholly tranquil
for a second before it buzzed off again

I said yesterday the signs were many
you said perhaps I'd seen
too many millimoles
of someone else's life

that anyone passing through
might own a share in
someone else's dying

I said that too
a Jewish doctor from Waco
told me years ago
"Sometimes people survive in spite of us"

I DREAMED YOU

a shrine of two
one who's visited for a vow

and one who floats on water as glow

whether visitor or visited
love astounds me

as if you were some higher form
of what I've lost and then returns to me

when the curtain's lifted

I climb your hands
my body falls as glass my soul's up in fragrance

some climbing is ascension
some is collapse

I dreamed you
combust the earth without catalyst

some eyes are mirrors
some mirrors are dust

38, 7, 31, 4

I was twelve years, nine months, and nineteen days old when
I heard the news, saw the footage. Were I already thirteen I
might have skipped the event the way hospitals skip a floor
that bears the dreaded number. O Maimonides, God's mercy,
Ya Ali, the Last Supper and the lunation, the dead were
held in unsensed space, unnameable bloating away blackened,
bouncing back and forth, from floor to ceiling, in zero gravity
without elevator stop. In hotels it's the same. Though there
the floor is the domain of fire. There was no hotel in the
camp but there was a hospital. I didn't need to be there. The
photographs, the brief video, my eyes dashing between screen
and my parents standing in a silence that drove them out of
the room as if they'd watched their bodies decompose. I didn't
step over the corpses or love Blake's fly. I'd seen flies swarm
the butcher's shop by then. You can't swat away what drowns
the buzzing before slaughter. Twelve years, six months, and
twenty-seven days later I was alone in my parents' bedroom in
Clarksville, Tennessee, when the dead reappeared. That same
old woman in her headscarf and housedress was screaming.
She looked older than heaven and hell and was wailing into
the camera. "Where is everyone?" In the footage, she's suspended,
her grief stuck on repeat, and I began my sobbing. I stood in line.
The line was long. I was way in the back. Burial foundation
six boulders deep then off to the core. How many floors to the
molten base? Does belonging still go on down there or is there
a red-light district to window-shop the poses of the massacred?
O Mohammad, Ya Ali, twelve years, two months, and seven
days later a door opened. I was somewhere and someone.

TRADITIONAL ANGER (IN THE SONORA)

Because you wait for what you asked for
how lonely is pleasure?

The saguaros want to speak
like daft telephone poles

more numerous closer apart
untransmittable

For there's water where there's no rain
and that after protracted

hours to explain
our bonds our pathways our molecules

water is water
is nothing more than life

And if you come
hydroelectric damned and saccadic

flooded plain and artificial
natural your claim

a carbon your every fission
an I

ALMOST YOUR LIFE

Then another fled resemblance and this
an ancient poet confirmed
as a bird of prey

hovered overhead when the after-rain
had summoned the reed beds
to disperse their taste

O what wit witness
"our killers have returned and you
stranger ask strange questions"

the snail of reparation
isn't the snail of forgiveness
carrying home on her back

a howdah where love is made
to a camel's cadence

Polyglot
in which language do you dream
and in which
will we speak in heaven

with reed beds by the sea
whose wind burqaed your eyes
and mouth with your hair

the sea that almost took your life
almost returned it

CORONA RADIATA

To erase myself   I erase myself

quiet silent mute   clay fire light

cold shadow sun   sorrow meadow wild

river sea land   drunk sober want

seize release expunge   part splice plunge

sound ear mouth   word would world

SPHINX POEM

The magnolia in our front yard had barely looped ten orbits
around the sun when we moved in. No Deep South
magnolia this Texas variety. In Atlanta

an ancient magnolia stood at the center of a hospital
for healing to depend on. The poison,
biohazard waste, blood at the roots.

If the windows were open
you could reach out, run
your pads over its wax without your tiptoes
calling on your cerebellum to intervene.

And when in bloom
the tree put on its Milky Way citrus bouquet
that had survived the extinction
dinosaurs couldn't. To exist

before bees did, to befriend
the primeval beetle and withstand
the weight of the gauche insect

with sheathed wings, the tree offered giant
armored flowers. ("Sheathed wings," *elytra*, Minecraft,
the sandbox that kidnaps children
and eats them.) Years later

after routine vampiric checkup in clinic, our friends
who lived in the historic district and had a glorious
magnolia percuss their windows on the second floor,

found out their son had mild lead toxicity.
Historic pipes moved them
out. We lost

our visitation rights with the grand Talauma. In 1703
while in Martinique, Charles Plumier
renamed the magnolia tree after his countryman
Pierre Magnol, the father

of modern botanic classification.
Then another father, nomenclatorial whiz
Carl Linnaeus, honored Charles

by renaming a tree plumeria.
The Frangipani, powerful
Roman family that gave of its own bread

to the people during a famine, and later stood behind
a Pope's investiture, also extracted perfume
from the flower, and possibly gave us Dante.

All around the world the frangipani goes by other names.
The champa, the egg yolk tree
fools its moth, the sphinx moth, the hummingbird

and hawkmoth (a Nabokov favorite).
Melia's bloom is nectarless. Its intense scent
inebriates the sphinx into pollinating it

with a proboscis gone fly fishing.
The tree thinks the high a fair trade
and the moth goes away hungry.

I LOVE MY LIFE

cheating on death
my kite a dragonfly
tied to a spider's thread

the spider that swallowed a caterpillar
that had lassoed herself in silk

I paint a rock
with crusty lichen, leprous
granular bacterial blue
in merger with fungus

and dream dreams
that harm no one

I love my life
cheating on death
tragedy can't tell

my terror from your pain
grief's brief allele
or methyl twigs
from helical switches

And the bovine
after milk and meat
who give of their lives to my teeth

their enamel my jaws
I sit at the table

MY SHAKESPEARE

Perfect translators that aliens are
this can't be the government of my exit.

It's time I changed my mask, time
that flings what it authors and what illusion conquers

extends a ladder to image
but only the heart contains: "White

what remains mine, white what I lose,"
the thought kills that you're not thought

and that I'm your beauty's in black.
With your body I filled my line, still

the soil's that I do common grow.
My exterior, which nature stores

as a map is stored, deserves a plaque:
the mask I wear, the kingdom that I owe.

FOOTNOTES IN THE ORDER OF DISAPPEARANCE

A fever of thyself think of the Earth

I call the finding of certain things loss

I hold grief close to brace myself for the expected

The unexpected not coeval with the unwanted
they kneel me

I have a fever

when at customs I don't declare
what I brought into my country from that other minor country

a periodic fever

when in legacy mode my teeth have grown
too yellow for the abrupt hug
of a carnivorous flower

And that I pray for bipedal aliens
or play to inner ear bones those Max Ernst structures

Consanguineous or not
all my erasures are relatives

And you and I are hapten-stance:
you elicit me to me
move me in me

I have a fever others speak I learned love in

For relief I braid Tylenol with Motrin
at the shore of words the sea ends

Consider me a color
an unspoken sound
aphasia won't clarify

Per your mother
they have books on tape now

Per mine dead dogs will follow me

The soul of one dog will enter and exit other dogs
whose deaths I'll come upon

I won't know whose soul I will run
lizards and rodents and a rabbit
will mortgage my dreams

There will be light to wake me sootless
there will be light to resect my spleen

There are always women and bees
and who can't tell a story about honey?

Newborns aside
I'm unlikely to cause anyone harm

My benefits outstrip my collateral
on an earth we'll never plow

What if butterfly or moth on lemon or mango tree?
What if I taste the coffee you swirled inside your cheeks?

To each its caterpillar

I defervesce
I have a fever others speak I learned love in

Between my nipples and knees and within
the frame whose borders are laser-hung
to render umpires surplus

I defervesce
our error was mutual
and being touched was how
you touched me back

Your cherries are black
your eyes grabbed mine by the elbows
our fourth and sixth cranial nerves intact

You pitched your face in my shoulder
variance in clinical features
strapped to the waist

To be clear
one mustn't be connected to the bed of another
about to be shocked

To be clear
what one does with the towel is the business
of making cancer history

A remittent fever
I too shall overcome

the majority incarcerated in herniated prisms
out of what kind of house into prison

Out of prison into what kind of house

My fever says I am the one who never was
a narcissus under hooves
now a boxthorn

I'd bury my sorrow alive
but my sorrow has bones

My fever says I need skin
other than that of a bacteriophage
and besides

mist was falling
and Sisyphus
forget him

he could've died like the rest of us

Where is he now
and what has he seen?
Which protection program and was he
at any point a Gizmo?

Tell me a story when you were little

Your mom bathed you until you were ten
you said you'd tie your dad's shoes
for him when he's ninety

Tell me when you opened your lunch box
she'd packed for you the night before

Here's a lock of your toddler hair
and your baby teeth

biting your dorsal wrist
in a perfect circle to tell the time

the marks take to disappear

{ }

ACKNOWLEDGMENTS AND NOTES

Special gratitude to the editors of the following publications in which the following poems appeared, sometimes in slightly different versions:

32 Poems: "The Living Are the Minority," "I, the Sole Witness to My Despair, Declare" ("Meditation? I can't tell my Buddhist prayers")
A Public Space: "Epithalamion"
Copper Nickel: "Tricolor," "In a Cemetery under a Solitary Walnut Tree That Crows"
Fence: "Kohl"
Green Linden: "Horses," "Corona Radiata"
Harvard Review: "Poem for Godot," "38, 7, 31, 4"
Kenyon Review: "Progress Notes," "Traditional Anger (in the Sonora)"
Los Angeles Review of Books: "The Scream," "Sphinx Poem"
Michigan Quarterly Review: "The Magic of Apricot", "Footnotes in the Order of Disappearance" ("I call the finding of certain things loss").
New England Review: "Bloodline" (as "Indigo")
Normal School: "Beanstalk"
One: "Footnotes to a Song"
Plume: "1ˢᵗ Love"
Poetry: "Plethora," "Nonterminal," "The Floor Is Yours"
Poetry Now: "National Park"
Prairie Schooner: "Tea and Sage"
New York Times Magazine: "Almost Your Life"
Scoundrel Time: "An Algebra Come Home," "After No Language," "Alignment," and "Body of Meaning"
Social Text: "Thank You," "Footnotes in the Order of Disappearance" ("That syphilis leads")

Sukoon: "Echo #1," "Maqam of Palm Trees," "Chamber Music"
Tongue Journal: "In the Garden," "I, the Sole Witness to My
Despair, Declare" ("Meditation? I search for a clown I kill")
The White Review: "Europa and the Bull," "Palestine, Texas"
The Wolf: "Colored Rings"
World Literature Today: "After Wine," "Last Night's Fever, This
Morning's Murder"

Sagittal Views is a collaborative work with my remarkable
friend Golan Haji, a Syrian Kurdish poet, translator, and
essayist who writes in Arabic. Golan left Syria in 2011 and
lives in Paris with his wife and daughter. The poems in *Sagittal
Views* are based on our meetings, phone conversations, and
email correspondence in Arabic. The proportion of "original
work" per author varies from poem to poem. Their form and
diction in English are mine.

"Progress Notes" was selected for *Best American Poetry 2017*.
"Corona Radiata" was selected for the broadside series of
Green Linden Press.

"Palestine, Texas" is included in the forthcoming anthology
Gracious: Contemporary Poems in the 21st Century South.

Many thanks to these journals and institutions for commis-
sioning or publishing pieces that became the organs of other
later poems: *Columbia Journal*, *Harvard Advocate*, *Los Angeles
Review of Books Online*, *Mantis*, *OmniVerse*, *Plume*, Poets.org, Po-
etry Society of America, Rubin Museum of Art, and Terezin
Music Foundation. Special thanks for the Lannan Founda-
tion, whose residency helped to start this project, and for the
Simon Guggenheim Foundation, whose fellowship helped to
complete it.

"The Magic of Apricot" was inspired by Mona Hatoum's exhibit at the Tate Modern.

"Maqam of Palm Trees" is for Iraqi musician and composer Rahim Alhaj.

"Epithalamion" was cowritten with Deema Shehabi on the event of Kafah and Dan's wedding.

"An Algebra Come Home" is for Marilyn Hacker.

"Bloodline" owes its existence to Kafah Bachari, Lazaro Cherem, Lyn Randolph, and Herbert Fred (to whom the poem's final line belongs).

"Footnotes to a Picture" concerns Walt Whitman.

In "Kohl," lines seven through ten are adaptations from classical Arabic poetry.

"Jigar" in "Last Night's Fever, This Morning's Murder" is Gigerxwin (nom de plume), the Syrian Kurdish poet who wrote in Kurmanji. He died in exile in Stockholm, and was buried in his house's courtyard in Qamishli, not far from where "Amira" lost her life.

The quote in "Alignment" belongs to an-Niffari.

The quotes in "Echo #14" belong to al-Hallaj.

"I Dreamed You" is an adaptation of my translation of Hussein Barghouthi's poem of the same title. The translation first appeared in *New American Writing*.

The quote in "My Shakespeare" is Paul Celan's (my translation from the Arabic).

The epigraph to the book's last poem is from Keats's *The Fall of Hyperion*.

I am greatly indebted to my colleagues (Ron, Mark, Lubna, Jamuna, Chau, and Roy) at the Medical Center Associates of Houston for accommodating me. And to the many friends and writers who made this manuscript better via various means: Latif Adnan, Hadeel Assali, Hayan Charara, Nick Flynn, Tonya Foster, Farid Matuk, Chris Martin, Sandeep Parmar, Hilary Plum, Phil Metres, Roger Reeves, Solmaz Sharif, Martha Serpas, Geroge Szirtes, Mary Szybist, and Zoe Wool.

Thank you, Wayne Miller and Daniel Slager. Thank you, Deema Shehabi and Marilyn Hacker.

Thank you, Golan Haji.

My greatest gratitude and love go to my Hana, Mona, and Ziyad.

Cybele Knowles

FADY JOUDAH has published three books of poems, *The Earth in the Attic, Alight,* and *Textu,* a book-long sequence of short poems whose meter is based on cellphone character count. He has translated several collections of poetry from the Arabic. He was a winner of the Yale Series of Younger Poets competition in 2007 and has received a PEN award, a Banipal/TLS prize from the UK, the Griffin Poetry Prize, and a Guggenheim fellowship. He lives in Houston, with his wife and kids, where he practices internal medicine.

milkweed
EDITIONS

Founded as a nonprofit organization in 1980, Milkweed Editions is an independent publisher. Our mission is to identify, nurture, and publish transformative literature, and build an engaged community around it.

Milkweed Editions is based in Bdé Óta Othuŋwe (Minneapolis) within Mní Sota Makhočhe, the traditional homeland of the Dakhóta people. Residing here since time immemorial, Dakhóta people still call Mní Sota Makhočhe home, with four federally recognized Dakhóta nations and many more Dakhóta people residing in what is now the state of Minnesota. Due to continued legacies of colonization, genocide, and forced removal, generations of Dakhóta people remain disenfranchised from their traditional homeland. Presently, Mní Sota Makhočhe has become a refuge and home for many Indigenous nations and peoples, including seven federally recognized Ojibwe nations. We humbly encourage our readers to reflect upon the historical legacies held in the lands they occupy.

milkweed.org

Interior design by Mary Austin Speaker
Typeset in Jenson
by Mary Austin Speaker

Adobe Jenson was designed by Robert Slimbach for Adobe
and released in 1996. Slimbach based Jenson's roman styles
on a text face cut by fifteenth-century type designer Nicolas
Jenson, and its italics are based on type created by Ludovico
Vicentino degli Arrighi, a late fifteenth-century
papal scribe and type designer.

Printed in the USA
CPSIA information can be obtained
at www.ICGtesting.com
JSHW080003150824
68134JS00021B/2261